William Huntington

Spoils Taken From the Tower of London

.

William Huntington

Spoils Taken From the Tower of London

ISBN/EAN: 9783744733670

Printed in Europe, USA, Canada, Australia, Japan

Cover: Foto ©ninafisch / pixelio.de

More available books at **www.hansebooks.com**

TAKEN FROM THE

TOWER of LONDON,

WITHOUT

SIEGE, VIOLENCE, BLOODSHED, CONQUEST, or LOSS to the Owners.

IN A

LETTER to a FRIEND.

BY

WILLIAM HUNTINGTON, S.S.

MINISTER OF THE GOSPEL

AT PROVIDENCE CHAPEL, LITTLE TITCHFIELD-STREET;
AT MONKWELL-STREET CHAPEL, IN THE CITY;
AND AT RICHMOND, IN SURREY.

Moreover, I have given to thee one Portion above thy Brethren.
Gen. xlviii. 22.

LONDON:

Sold by G. Terry, Paternofter-row; J. Chalmers, N° 210, White-crofs-ftreet, near Moorfields; J. Davidfon, N° 7, Poftern-row, Tower-hill; Mr. Baker, N° 226, Oxford-ftreet; Mrs. Howes, N° 15, Charles-ftreet, Wells-ftreet; at Monkwell-ftreet Chapel every Tuefday evening; at Providence Chapel, Titchfield-ftreet; by Mr. Mantle, Lewes, Suffex; Mr. Fenley, Broad Mead, Briftol; and by Mr. Chamberlain, Portfmouth.

MDCCLXXXVIII.

[Price SIX-PENCE.]

S P O I L S

TAKEN FROM

THE TOWER.

From a certain *Loyalist* in the *Burning Bush*, to the *Son of David*, alias Mr. DAVIDSON, No. 7, *Postern Row*, secured by a *Wall*, though in view of the *Ditch*, living near the *Tower*.

DEAR SIR,

I WISH grace, mercy, and peace to be for ever with thee through Jesus Christ, our most blessed God and Saviour. In my way home, after you was so kind as to accompany me in viewing the many curiosities in the Tower, I fell to considering and spiritualizing the various things that I had seen; and upon reflection my roving fancy took her flight, and at her return many things were exhibited on the threshold; the conclusion I made is; that your situation is somewhat singular, and your privileges such as few can boast of.

You live in daily prospect of the *high tower*, Psa. xviii. 2. which the royal psalmist, though

highly

highly favoured of God, was not always indulged with. When we are fixed on the high tower the world appears as the drop of a bucket, or the small duft of a balance, lighter than vanity and lefs than nothing. You know the promife is that the faint fhall dwell on high—that his place of defence fhall be the munition of rocks—that bread fhall be given him and his water fhall be fure—that he fhall fee the King in his beauty, and behold the land that is very far off.

The *royal armory* is within a *bowfhot* of your perfon, wherein there hang a *thoufand bucklers, all fhields of mighty men*, Cant. iv. 4. Many a good foldier of Jefus Chrift, when engaged in the fight of faith, has felt his need of the helmet of hope,—the breaft-plate of righteoufnefs,—the fhield of help,—the fhield of faith,—the girdle of truth,—and the fword of the Spirit, who never could fay, as you can, that they lived all the year round clofe to and in full view of the *royal armory.*

Nor have you any thing to fear from the *horfe armory.* The horfes, their armour, their formidable riders, and their weapons of war, ftrike no terror; they are all fixed, and confined in perpetual imprifonment—there is no apprehenfion of any danger from them; all the terror they have caufed in the land of the living is now over. What would thoufands of Chriftians have given to have feen the *Saracens* in the fame manner confined when they appeared fo terrible: as

it

it is written, " And the number of the army of
" the horſemen were two hundred thouſand
" thouſand : And I heard the number of them.
" And thus I ſaw the horſes in the viſion, and
" them that ſat on them, having breaſt-plates
" of fire, and of jacinct, and brimſtone ; and the
" heads of the horſes were as the heads of lyons,
" and out of their mouths iſſued fire, ſmoke,
" and brimſtone. By theſe three was the third
" part of men killed," Rev. ix. 16—18. Thus
the Tower preſents ſome things in effigy which
John ſaw in viſion ; and the iron breaſt-plates on
the Saracens troop horſes were lively emblems
of the feared conciences of that troop of locuſts
who ſpread the doctrines of the Turkiſh alcoran ;
and of the trading ſwarm of Popiſh prieſts, who
get money for themſelves, and ſouls for the devil,
by ſelling bulls and pardons.

Many a young Chriſtian who has had Chriſt
in him the hope of glory, has been afraid at firſt
to launch out into the world in a public pro-
feſſion, *ſaying, with the ſluggard, there is a lion
without, I ſhall be ſlain in the ſtreets,* Prov. xxii. 13.
whereas you can go every day and ſee not only
the lions, but wolves, bears, tygers, and leo-
pards, all confined in their dens ; yea, you can
lay on your bed and hear their terrible roar, but
not one of them can come nigh thy dwelling.
Highly favoured Daniel, only for calling upon
his God, was caſt in among them ; but as he
cleaved cloſe to the lion of the tribe of Judah,

the others could do him no mifchief. O what a
day will that be, when the *lion of the bottomlefs pit*
fhall be as clofely cooped as thofe are in the
Tower. The angel will come down at the time
appointed, and bring his chain in his hand—
lay hold of that old ferpent the Devil, and
bind him a thoufand years, caft him into the
pit, and fet a feal upon him, which will make
the den more fecure than the feal of the king of
Babylon made that of the lions den, that his
purpofe might not be changed concerning Da-
ñiel; or the feal of the Jewifh rabbies on the
Saviour's fepulchre, which was intended to baffle
the force of Omnipotence.

The *Tower-ditch* may ferve to remind thee of
the very many who by miffing the way to the
ftreight gate have been directed farther from it by
blind guides, who have groped for the wall till
the leader and the led have both fell into the
ditch together. Two or three perfons have fell
into the Tower-ditch in thy days; but it is to
be feared there are many more who daily fall
into a ditch far worfe and far deeper than that.
But there is a wall between thee and the ditch,
though but a very low one—which may ferve to
remind thee of Zion's fafety; in that day fhall
this fong be fung, We have a ftrong city, falvation will God appoint for walls and bulwarks.
Souls encompaffed with thefe are well fecured
from the ditch. The wall being fo very low on
the hill fide, and fo high on the fide of the
ditch,

ditch, ferves to fhew us the fide on which the mifer takes a view of his bags, *whofe wealth is his ftrong city, and as an high wall in his own conceit,* Prov. xviii. 11. fo the outward Tower wall appears to a perfon on the ditch fide; but was he upon Tower-hill it would harldly be feen; fo let a worldling be ftationed on Zion-hill, and his wall vanifhes altogether, and appears lefs than nothing. But to fet a man here is the work of him who faid to the Publican, *This day is falvation come to this houfe*; upon the proclamation of which the wall of wealth yielded up the fort of the heart, and the root of all evil was no longer a bulwark of fafety.

You have a confiderable number of men under arms near your dwelling both day and night; whereas Zion and her rightful fovereign have but few if any more who keep guard round their royal ftate bed: *Behold his bed which is Solomon's; threefcore valiant men are about it, of the valiant of Ifrael. They all hold fwords, being expert in war; every man hath his fword upon his thigh, becaufe of fear in the night,* Song iii. 7, 8. This guard may ferve to remind thee of the minifters of the gofpel, who are to defend the truth, and the church of the living God, which is the ground and pillar of it, with fuch fpiritual weapons as the Lord's armory furnifhes them with. But thy fure defence is in the God of armies, who is both our guardian and our watch; *unlefs the Lord keep the city, the watchman waketh but in vain.*

If

If I miſtake not, thy dwelling is between two hills; one is called *Great* and the other *Little Tower Hill.* It is a bleſſed thing to have one's dwelling among the hills; that is, to have the ancient mountain of ETERNAL ELECTION made ſure behind, and the everlaſting hill of GLORI-FICATION in full view before. It is prophecied that *the mountains ſhall bring peace to the people, and the little hills by righteouſneſs*, Pſa. lxxii. 3. upon theſe God has promiſed ſhowers of bleſſings, which make the heart ſoft, and cauſe joy unſpeakable to ſpring up within; this crowns a goſpel year with goodneſs, while God's paths drop fatneſs—they drop upon the paſtures of the wilderneſs, *and the little hills rejoice on every ſide*, Pſalm lxv. 11, 12.

The *royal crown* may ſerve to remind thee of the *crown of knowledge* with which the prudent are crowned;—of the *crown of loving kindneſs and tender mercies* which the believer appears in on certain court days;—of the *crown of life* promiſ-ed to the faithful overcomer at his death;—of the *crown of righteouſneſs* which is to be worn by kings and prieſts when they will appear as faithful witneſſes at the day of judgment;—and of the *incorruptable crown of glory* that is undefiled, and that never fades away, reſerved in heaven for thoſe who are kept by the mighty power of God through faith to ſalvation. He *whoſe eyes are as a flame of fire, and on whoſe head are many crowns*, Rev. xix. 13. will one day or other bring theſe

forth

forth in all their divine luftre; when the chofen fraternity are raifed up *from the duft, and the beggars from the dunghill, and made to fit among princes, and to inherit the throne of glory.* 1 Sam. ii. 8.

The *royal diadem* with its numerous gems brought to my mind the inconceivable beauty, and the fparkling luftre of divine majefty, that the ever bleffed Saviour, the Prince of Peace, fometimes appears in, when he comes to pay his addreffes or love vifits to poor wretched finners, in order to woo and efpoufe them to himfelf. *In thofe* nuptial days, *the Lord of Hofts is a crown of glory and a diadem of beauty to the refidue of his people,* Ifai. xxviii. 5. Nor will Zion be lefs in the eyes of her royal bridegroom when he rifes and fhines with all his glorious majefty on her; fhe will be a *royal diadem in the hand of her God, and be no more termed forfaker or defolate, but Hephzibah, the Lord's delight.* Ifai. lxii. 3, 4. To be bleffed with a favory experience of this, and to enjoy the Spirit's fweet influences, are fummary pledges and foretaftes of what is to come; thefe are the *marks that fecure the* PRIZE *of the high calling of God in* •*Chrift Jefus.* The foul that knows, experiences, and enjoys thefe things, and is perfuaded in his own mind (by the Spirit of faith) of the reality of them, and of his part and lot in them, may fay, as Job did, *My judgment is as a robe and a diadem.* Job xxix. 14.

The *golden fceptre* may remind thee of the fceptre of righteoufnefs, by which every faithful fubject

ject of the King of Kings is ruled. Victory over
devils, the world, felf, fin, and death, is the
bleffed effect of being under the fceptre of righteoufnefs and the dominion of grace. It is true,
none of thefe adverfaries are deftroyed in the
ftricteft fenfe; but their deftroying power is with
refpect to the elect, and they will be all beat
down under our feet in due time. I am an eye
witnefs that you touched the golden fceptre once;
but this is not enough, we muft appear at court
daily to renew our friendfhip, and give proof of
our loyalty. Beware of a fhynefs—a diftance—a
lukewarmnefs—indulged fins—contracted guilt
—an accufing devil—or, what is worfe than all,
an accufing confcience getting between the King
and thee; thefe things obfcure or bring a cloud
over the throne of grace, which in time hinders
prayer from going forth. At the worft of times,
and with the worft of cafes, do as fome did in
the days of old, who faid, *I will go in and ftand
before the King, and if I perifh I perifh*; to whom
the golden fceptre was held out, and half the
kingdom promifed; but Chrift gives more, for
the whole kingdom is ours.

The curtana or blunt fword of mercy, which is car-
ried between the two fwords of juftice, the fpiritual and the temporal, brought to my mind the
terrible appearance that the Lord makes when he
firft comes to the chofen finner and wounds him
with the fword of the Spirit, which feparates
joints and marrow and difcovers the receffes of
the

the heart, infomuch that the poor finner thinks
he is going to deftruction; whereas the *fword of
mercy,* though it hath got two edges, yet it hath
no point. The wound or rather bruife that the
Saviour gives us with this, when he appears as
conqueror, ferves to make more work for him as
a phyfician. I wound and I heal, faith the blefled Redeemer; the Lord maketh fore and bind-
eth up; he that *girds his fword upon his thigh as
the* moft mighty, is *anointed to bind up the broken
hearted and to fet at liberty thofe that are bruifed.*
Luke iv. 18. I think this blunt fword may reprefent that which Mofes fpeaks of; *Happy art
thou O Ifrael; who is like unto thee, O people faved by
the Lord, the fhield of thy help, and who is the* SWORD
OF THINE EXCELLENCY. Deut. xxxiii. 29. An excellent fword this, there is none like it; the
wounds we receive from this are excellent, noble,
divine, and durable; God grant they never may
be healed while we live in the world, feeing a
broken fpirit is an acceptable facrifice; under
every wound remember it is the fword of mercy;
in mercy it is ufed, and through mercy it will do
no hurt; mercy has a foft hand, a tender heart,
and compaffionate bowels; if fatherly feverity
gives a wound, tender pity applies the balm. It
may be faid of a faint in a good fenfe as it is faid
of the Popifh beaft in a bad one; *That he received
a wound by a fword and did live, for his deadly wound
was healed*; and the whole world will one day
wonder as much at the faint, as it wondered after
the

the beaſt. In ſhort, it will not be terrible to a child of God to die of the wounds given by the ſword of mercy. This weapon is generally uſed where peace is proclaimed; *there is that ſpeaketh like the piercing of a ſword, but the tongue of the wiſe is health.* Prov. xii. 18.

The *ivory ſceptre with the dove on the top* put me in mind of Solomon's ivory throne, which that peaceable prince made for himſelf, *overlayed with the beſt gold; the throne had ſix ſteps, and the top of the throne was round behind; and there were ſtays on either ſide of the place on the ſeat, and two lions ſtood beſide the ſtays; and twelve lions ſtood there on the one ſide and one the other upon the ſix ſteps; there was not the like made in any kingdom.* 1 Kings x. 18—20. This throne beautifully typified the throne of grace; the light colour may ſhew the Saviour's holy and merciful proceedings with his own peo-ple; the two lions at the foot of the throne, the one repreſenting the terrible majeſty of his deity— *the lion hath roared who will not fear, God hath ſpoken who can but prophecy?* the other the majeſty of his riſen, exalted, and glorifi:d humanity, he being the *lion of the tribe of Judah.* The ſix ſteps may prefigure the Saviour's way to his throne; he went to it, 1ſt. By his deſcent from heaven; 2dly. By his aſſumption of human nature; 3dly. By his ſtate of humiliation as a ſervant; 4thly. By his obedient deſcent by death into the grave; 5thly. By his reſurrection; and 6thly. By his aſ-cenſion to heaven, where he is ſat down on the
throne

throne of majefty on high. The twelve lions on the fteps of the ivory throne might reprefent not only the twelve tribes, who at firft fupported Solomon on his throne, but the twelve apoftles, who as prime minifters of ftate, and the honourable privy council of the great king, appeared bold, valiant, and courageous, fpent all they had, and were fpent themfelves in defending the honour, hereditary and meritorious right of their royal mafter to thet hrone of David, and the government of the houfe of Ifrael; their ftanding on the fteps may denote their afcenfion after their mafter, and the impoffibility of any getting to the Saviour but by obedience to the doctrines which they taught; it may likewife denote their afcenfion to be with their Lord, who will one day appear *twelve lions* indeed, when they fit on twelve thrones judging the twelve tribes of Ifrael. The *ivory fceptre* put me in mind of the fceptre fwayed by the Saviour in glory; he is king of Zion and king of glory, king of faints and king of angels, principalities and powers. The colour of this fceptre put me in mind of the bright, the glorious, and lovely proceedings of the great king among the fpirits of juft men made perfect.

The *dove upon the top,* the *emblem of peace,* ferved to remind me of thofe peaceable manfions and quiet habitations above, where uninterrupted peace fhall be enjoyed, the wicked ceafe from troubling, and the weary be for ever at reft. The dove brought to my mind the bleffed Spirit of God,

God,

God, which refts upon every loyal fubject of the
Saviour's fpiritual kingdom; and on which account the church is called by her royal bridegroom, *My love, my dove, my undefiled*; *my dove*
that dwells in the cleft of the rock, Let me hear thy
voice, fays the altogether lovely, *Let me fee thy*
countenance; *fweet is thy voice and thy countenance is*
comely.

The *filver fountain* being empty put me in
mind of the emptinefs of all fublunary enjoyments, which at firft fight feem to promife much,
but afford no more than the fountain did to us,
that is, the beholding of it with our eyes which are
never fatisfied with feeing. An *empty fountain*
feems a contradiction in terms, becaufe it has no
fupply from itfelf; it fhould rather be called a
ciftern, becaufe it will hold water if you put it
into it; but all the tranfient enjoyments of this
world are in a ciftern that can hold no water.
My people, faith God, have committed two evils,
they have forfaken me the *fountain of living* water
and hewed out to themfelves cifterns, broken
cifterns that can hold no water.   God is a fountain of living water, from whom through the
Lamb comes that glorious river, the ftreams
whereof make glad the city of God; fouls filled
and fatisfied with this water never thirft· for the
vanities of this world again; he has got a fpring
within him, as wifdom fays, *a good man is fatisfied*
from himfelf, that is, from a knowledge of his own
fafety

fafety and happinefs, for his very heart is a fountain, being partaker of that water that fprings
up into everlafting life; on which account the
church is called *a garden enclofed, a fpring fhut up,
and a fountain fealed.* This fpring fhall carry us
at laft into that inexhauftable fountain from
whence the ftreams defcend; then we fhall be
abundantly *fatisfied with the goodnefs of his houfe,
and drink of the river of his pleafure; for with him
is the fountain of life;* until which happy and
blefled period we muft content ourfelves with
that glorious declaration that heaven has made
to Zion—ALL MY SPRINGS ARE IN THEE.

The *golden eagle* with her expanded wings put
me in mind of the amazing condefcenfion and
tender love of God, which quickens, enflames,
and bears the church above the world. Mofes
reprefents this bird as turning over her eggs, that
they may all get warm alike; as hovering over
her young, and taking them on her wings and
mounting up with them, in order to teach them
how to fly; and then compares it to the tender
care and love of God to his people: " As an
" eagle ftirreth up her neft, fluttereth over her
" young, fpreadeth abroad her wings, taketh
" them, beareth them on her wings; fo the Lord
" alone did lead Jacob, and there was no ftrange
" God with him: He made him ride on the
" high places of the earth," Deut. xxxii. 11—13.

The eagle is a very towering flyer, noted for
fcent and quicknefs of fight; on which account
heavenly-

heavenly-minded fouls are compared to her;
" they fhall mount up as upon eagles wings,
" they fhall run and not be weary, they fhall
" walk and not faint." Job fays the *eagle be-
holds afar off*; and I am fure the eye of faith fees
farther than all the eagles in the world; the
antient faints faw the promife at a diftance;
Enoch the feventh from Adam faw the day of
judgment; and the eye of faith will pry into
heaven itfelf, and fee the way thither; fo that
the eye of faith exceeds the eye of the eagle, for
that is a path that no *fowl knoweth, and which the
vulture's eye hath never feen.* It is faid of the eagle
that fhe can look at the full blaze of the fun;
fo can the Chriftian, when the *Sun has looken upon
him*; he can fee him that is invifible, and find
his fight ftrengthened inftead of weakened—it
affords pleafure inftead of pain; it *is a precious
thing for the eyes to behold the fun.*

We were informed that the holy oil is put into
the golden eagle, and poured out of its beak
into the golden fpoon, with which the kings of
Great Britain are anointed; that put me in mind
of the *golden pipes, which empty the golden oil out of
themfelves,* Zech. iv. 12. The *candleftick* reprefents the church; the *bowl* upon the top of it the
gofpel of Chrift preached; the *feven lamps* the
eyes of the Lord upon it, and his precious falvation in it; the *feven pipes* reprefent tried, pu-
rified, and faithful minifters, who are minifters
of the fpirit; who being anointed with the *oil of*

joy

joy themselves, *anoint others with the same oil in the name of the Lord,* Zech. iv. 2. James v. 14. and all this comes from Him who is said to bear Jacob as on eagles wings, who was *anointed with the oil of gladness above his fellows.* Pf. xlv. 7. that he might give us *beauty for ashes, the oil of joy for mourning, and the garment of praise for the spirit of heaviness,* Ifa. lxi. 3. This anointing makes us kings and priests unto God. This oil makes the countenance of a faint to shine; it keeps the lamp of his falvation burning with *love, light,* and *zeal,* fo that it goeth not out by night, nor even at midnight; " the light of the righteous rejoiceth, when the lamp of the wicked is put out." There is a *treasure to be desired,* faith the wife man, *and it is oil in the dwelling of the wife;* which will certainly be fulfilled when the foolish virgins will fay to the wife, Give us of your oil, for our lamps are gone out. This oil is no lefs than the Holy Ghoft, the Spirit of all grace. Jefus was anointed with the Holy Ghoft. The foul that has got this blessing shall find all things work for his good; " let the righteous fmite him, it shall be a kindnefs; let him reprove him, it shall be an excellent oil." Job was no ftranger to this when he made this doleful and lamentable complaint: " O that I were as in " months paft, as in the days when God pre- " ferved me; when his candle shined upon my " head, and when by his light I walked through " darknefs; as I was in the days of my youth,

" when

" when the fecret of God was upon my taber-
" nacle; when the Almighty was yet with me;
" when my children were about me; when I
" wafhed my fteps with butter, and the rock
" poured me out rivers of oil," *Job* xxix. 2—6.

The *golden fpoon* may ferve to caution us againft remiffnefs in duty, coldnefs, flothfulnefs, and negligence in the ways of God, which make Chriftians weak, fickly, and childifh in fpiritual things. Spoons are table furniture, generally ufed to feed children; we are commanded to grow in grace and knowledge—to be men in underftanding. A ftunted, weak, rickety child is always in the cradle, the chair, the arms, the fwing, the back-ftring, or the go-cart; they are always in danger—never out of harm's way. Paul fpeaks of the Hebrews, who for the time they had made a profeffion ought to have been teachers, who needed teaching again—being children—needing milk inftead of meat; he that ufeth milk, fays the apoftle, is unfkilful in the word of righteoufnefs—for he is a babe. It is to our own advantage that we grow in knowledge and experience; we are then able to give a reafon of our hope, defend our own teftimony, ftop the mouth of a gainfayer, and difcover the emptinefs of a fawning hypocrite. It is by trials, by watchfulnefs, by diligence, by meditation, by reading, by fpiritual converfation, and by prayer, that Chriftians *grow as the vine, revive as the corn,* and flourifh as the palm tree. Such fouls are capable of difcerning, receiving, and digefting ftrong and wholefome doctrines, which the apoftle calls meat. " I have fed you (faith " he) with milk, not with meat, for ye were not " able to bear it, nor yet now are ye able; " ftrong meat is for them of full age, who by " reafon of ufe have their fenfes exercifed to " difcern between good and evil." If my friend can bear fuch food as this, there is another cu- riofity that may be confidered, and that is

The *golden faltcellar of ftate*, made like the fquare white tower, which is ufed at the king's table on the day of coronation. This golden faltcellar may prefigure a believing heart blefled with the grace of God, which will preferve us to God's everlafting kingdom: *Have falt in your- felves*, fays the Saviour, *and have peace one with another*, Mark ix. 50. Every fpiritual facrifice ftands in need of this favory article. The facri- fices of a broken heart, of prayer, of praife, of alms-giving, of thankfgiving, yea, and even the *body which is to be prefented as a living facrifice*, ftands in need of falt: " Every oblation of thy " meat-offering fhalt thou feafon with falt; nei- " ther fhalt thou fuffer the falt of the covenant " of thy God to be lacking from thy meat- " offerings; with all thine offerings thou fhalt " offer falt," *Levit. ii. 13. Every facrifice fhall be falted with falt*, Mark ix. 49. The apoftles and Jewifh difciples were the falt of the land of Ca- naan; *ye are the falt of the earth*, Matt. v. 13.—

and

and fo the Jews found it at the deftruction of
Jerufalem. When the Chriftians fled to *Pella* in
Caelo Syria, the Jews had loft all their feafoning,
and their favour, and they became a ftink in the
noftrils of God, and he numbered them to the
fword, till they ftank upon the earth.

Salt is a prefervative, and of a communica-
tive nature; fo divine grace faves a man, and
ferves to feafon others; without this a man is
nothing; without this he can be of no fpiritual
ufe or advantage to others: *Let your fpeech be
always with grace, feafoned with falt, that ye may
know how ye ought to anfwer every man*, Col. iv. 6.
It is this favory article that makes the difference
between a real Chriftian and a hypocrite; the
latter may learn the language of a Chriftian, his
outward deportment, and the form of religion,
and talk about a good and bad fpirit, as fome
do who know of no other fpirit than that of
fpirituous liquors; but thefe hypocrites cannot
counterfeit nor defcribe this falt; this feafoning
lies too deep for them, it can only be known by
experience, and defcribed by the experienced.
He that was inftrumental of making known the
favour of Chrift's name in every place, and was
a fweet favour unto God in them that are faved
and in them that perifh, could fay, *It is meet for
me to think this of you all—that ye are all partakers of
my grace*, Phil. i. 7. A wolf in fheep's clothing
may preach, converfe, or write, but he cannot
feafon; hypocrites may be pleafed and charmed
with

with words, for they don't know but what the kingdom of God is in word; we know that *salt is good, but with them it hath loft its favour;* they have no relifh for it, *therefore how fhall they be feafoned* with it? Luke xiv. 34. The true Chriftian looks more after the power than the found; he is more for favory meat than mufic: *Can that which is unfavory be eaten without falt,* fays Job, *or is there any tafte in the white of an egg? How forcible are right words, but what doth your arguing reprove,* Job vi. 6, 25.

The *golden bracelets* brought to my mind the fpiritual ornaments of the Jewifh church in her profperity; " I decked thee alfo with ornaments, " and I put bracelets upon thy hands, and a " chain on thy neck; I put jewels on thy fore- " head, and ear-rings in thine ears, and a beau- " tiful crown on thy head," *Ezek.* xvi. 11, 12. The beft royal *robe* that ever Zion put on is the *imputed righteoufnefs of Jefus Chrift;* the next to that is the *garment of falvation;* and under both thefe *the ornament of a meek and quiet fpirit, in the fight of God of great price.* The fineft and moft delicate hand is the hand of faith, by which the foul *lays hold on eternal life;* by this *the King of Heaven was held in the galleries,* Cant. vii. 5. with this the princefs royal held her adorable lover: *I held him faft, I would not let him go, until I had brought him into my mother's houfe and into the chamber of her that conceived me,* Song iii. 4. where the marriage treaty was fettled—*My beloved is mine and I am his.*

his. The beſt ſpiritual *bracelet* that I know of, is the bond of everlaſting love; this is the *bond* of *union* and the *bond* of all perfeĉtion, and is a *ring* for the finger. Luke xv. 22. a *chain* for the neck. Cant. iv. 9. and a *bracelet* for the wriſt. Ezek. xvi. 11. it is a ſure, a ſatisfaĉtory and an everlaſting token; it is the main tie of eternal wedlock, and the root of all the joys that attend it either in this world or in that which is to come. The hand of faith, however delicate in the eyes of ſome, is nothing without this ornament. 1 Cor. xiii. 2. *Faith worketh by love.* This ornament makes the ſpouſe appear an honour to her huſband and an honourable manager of her houſhold (her children riſe up and call her bleſſed). *Faith worketh by love,* and love is an helpmate to faith; *Charity believeth all things*; with this working hand the ſpouſe *maketh fine linen and ſelleth it, and delivers girdles of truth to ſpiritual merchants; ſtrength and honour are her clothing, and ſhe ſhall rejoice in time to come.* Prov. xxxi. 24, 25.

The *golden ſpurs* worn at the coronation may ſerve to caution us againſt ſlothfulneſs; we are commanded to run the race ſet before us, not to turn to the right hand or the left, not to look back or tarry in all the plain; Chriſtians are not compared to elephants or camels, but to horſes, harts, hinds, and roes; creatures that are ſwift a-foot. The ſpurs brought to my mind the cutting reproofs and rebukes that the lively and truly gracious chriſtian ſometimes gives to the ſluggiſh,

careleſs,

carelefs, and remifs profeffor. Solomon fays, *A reproof entereth more into a wife man than an hundred ftripes into a fool.* Prov. xvii. 10. A bright, fhining, diligent chriftian is a living reproof to the wicked, and a golden fpur to a fluggifh profeffor. Nothing is more mortifying to a *heavy jib horfe* than a good roweled fpur; you know *the flock of the houfe of Judah, that the Lord of hofts vifited, are called his goodly horfe in the battle.* Zach. x. 3. and troop horfes are feldom ridden without a provoking fpur; Paul fpeaks of the *liberal Corinthians, of whom he boafted to them of Macedonia, that fome in Achaia were ready a year ago, and that their zeal had provoked very many.* 2 Cor. ix. 2.

The moft difagreeable fight to me in all the Tower was what they call, the *fchool of apes.* This apifh academy, without a teacher, put me in mind of a band of hypocritical profeffors, who think to bribe heaven with a counterfeit fhew, and to pafs difguifed in fheep's clothing, though they are without Chrift in the world. Eliphaz fays, *The congregation of hypocrites fhall be defolate, and fire fhall confume the Tabernacles of bribery.* Job xv. 34. That *very large ape* that fat at the left hand corner as we entered the room, which took the other little ones into its hands, put them between its hinder legs, warmed them by the fire, hugged them in its arms, while all the little ones fat in awe with their eyes fixed, obferving nothing but the motions of him, had a very ftrange appearance. This lord paramount, which fat as a father

B 4 of

of the family, put me in mind of the devil's fondling and making sport of those of his own household, which the Saviour calls *the synagogue of Satan.* Rev. ii. 9. Christ says that *mammon* is the *master* of those mimickers of religion, who *draw near to God with their mouth while their hearts are far from him*; yea, he calls the devil the father of hypocrites; *Woe unto you scribes, pharisees, hypocrites,* Luke xi. 44. *Ye are of your father the devil, and the lusts of your father ye will do.* John viii. 44. Apes are noted for mimickry and activity; I have seen some of them mount over and tumble like a mountebank on a stage; you know the word *hypocrite* signifies a *mountebank* or *stage player* in scripture, who generally appears in the character of another instead of his own, as an hypocrite does in the character of a saint; hence the Saviour's caution, *Beware of false prophets, which come to you in sheeps clothing, but inwardly they are ravening wolves.* Matt. vii. 15. I considered the *school of apes* as lively emblems of Job's *congregation of hypocrites,* on the following accounts.

1st. They come the nighest to the human species of any of the brute creation; and of all the religious orders among men there is none come so near the *new creation,* or to souls *created anew in Christ Jesus* as a varnished hypocrite, who has laid by his written form of religion and counterfeits a spiritual worshipper.

2dly.

2dly. The ufe that the ape makes of its fore paws, which are fo much like the human hands, difplays the dexterity of the hypocrite, who can *weave the fpider's web* of felf-righteoufnefs, and *hatch the cockatrice egg* of ferpentine mifchief. Ifai. lxix. 5. even in the church of God. Hence wifdom compares the hypocrite to that fubtle weaver; and there is a kind of apes called the fpider ape; *The fpider taketh hold with her hands and is in king's palaces.* Prov. xxx. 28. and like the fpider, the hypocrite generally entangles him-felf in his own web; hence Bildad *declares the hypocrite's hope fhall perifh, that his hope fhall be cut off, and his truft fhall be in a fpider's web.* Job viii. 13, 14.

3dly. The fagacity of the ape which tries to imitate every thing that it fees a perfon do; fo the hypocrite imitates the faint. Does the chrif-tian enforce fpiritual holinefs? the hypocrite does the fame; but to what purpofe? if a man was to enforce obedience to the third commandment all the year round to me, yet if himfelf lived in blaf-phemy, I fhould hate him and lightly efteem his doctrine, as it appeared to have no influence on himfelf. It is common for hypocrites to make a great outcry againft the grace of God, and cry up the holy law as the only rule of life, while any difcerning eye may fee they privately hate and feek to injure the caufe of God; would fooner offend his fervants and worfhippers, than fpend one hour to reform the vile. This fhews their en-mity

mity againſt God, the pleaſure they take in the
triumphs they give the Philiſtines; beſides, pre-
cepts enforced by people abandoned to wickednefs, who live on, cohabit with, and ſtand as
pimps for private drunkards, what can be expected from them? when it is evident they are deſ-
titute of the grace of God, nurſes for hypocrites,
making a gain of godlineſs, living like drone bees
on the hive of the induſtrious, and eat the bread
of idleneſs. Reproofs or inſtructions given by
ſuch awful characters only harden rebels in their
ſins, and can have no more weight on a ſerious
perſon than the rebukes of Judas (whom the Saviour calls a devil) had, when he rebuked the
Saviour and Mary about the waſte of ointment;
no faint under the dominion of grace and in
union with Chriſt can ever ſlight the power of the
Spirit, by giving heed to an abuſed precept in
the mouth of a palpable impoſtor. We know
the grace of God teaches the faint to have reſpect
to all the commandments, the *fourth* as well as
the reſt; a precept in the mouth of a rebel is
like a parable in the mouth of a fool. *Six days*
ſhalt thou labour and do all thy work. Exod. xx. 9.
If any will not work neither ſhall he eat. 2 Theſſ. iii.
10. *If any provide not for his own*, and eſpecially
for thoſe of his own houſe, he *hath denied the faith and*
is worſe than an infidel. 1 Tim. v. 8. they are to
ſtudy to be quiet, to do their own buſineſs, and work
with their own hands. 1 Theſſ. iv. 11. If the hypocrite

pocrite denies the faith, how can he keep his credit up but by making a noife about the law? for it is the talker and the *hearer of the law that is juſtified by him,* not *the doer.* Rom. ii. 13. for he is an Antinomian.

4thly. The knowledge that thefe creatures feem to have of the different fexes of the human fpecies has fomething very fhocking and difguſtful in it. They are creatures noted for craftinefs, always in mifchief, ſtealing things and hiding them, and the feeming pleafure that they take in doing it, is emblematical enough of the lechery and treachery of hypocrites; witnefs the council of that arch monſter, that fworn enemy to God's Ifrael, namely Balaam, as it is written; and Mofes faid, *Have ye faved all the women alive?* Behold, thefe caufed the children of Ifrael, through the council of Balaam, to commit a trefpafs againſt the Lord in the matter of Peor. *Numb.* xxxi. 15, 16. Thus the devil got his end, through the inſtrumentality of wretched Balaam, which ended in the deſtruction of the *women of Moab* as well as the men of Ifrael. The effects of Balaam's council may be gathered from the following paſfage; And Ifrael abode in Shittem, and the people began to commit whoredom with the daughters of Moab. And they called the people to the facrifices of their gods; and the people did eat and bowed down to their gods. And Ifrael joined himfelf to Baalpeor; and the anger of the Lord was kindled againſt Ifrael. *Numb.* xxv. 1—3.

This

This old leaven lurked at the root of the Nicola-
tians, who taught community of wives, which
the Saviour complains of to the angel of the
church of Pergamus; *Thou haft them there that
hold the doctrine of Balaam, who taught Balack to
caft a ftumbling block before the children of Ifrael; fo
haft thou alfo them that hold the doctrine of the Nico-
latians, which thing I hate.* Rev. ii. 14, 15. We
know there is no *escaping the pollutions that are
in the world through luft,* but by the almighty
power and fovereign grace of God; it is true,
there is a NATION PURE IN THEIR OWN EYES, but
they are not fo in God's eyes till wafhed from
their filthinefs. The cunning, artful craftinefs,
the pilfering tricks, and the pleafure that the ape
takes in doing mifchief, brought to my mind the
fubtile proceedings of thofe profeffors which Jude
compares to *natural brute beafts, made to be taken
and deftroyed, who fpeak evil of the things that they
underftand not.* Jude x. They are faid to walk in
craftinefs and handle the word of God deceit-
fully. 2 Cor. iv. 2. Some of this ftamp came to
betray the Saviour, but he could penetrate into
their *craftinefs.* Luke xx. 23. The pleafure thofe
falfe profeffors take in doing mifchief to the caufe,
to the reputation, and ufefulnefs of the faints, by
giving offence to them, by ftaggering the weak,
by tripping up the heels of the feeker, by
ftrengthening the hands of evil doers, by em-
boldening the prefumptuous, fortifying the erro-
neous, and furnifhing the contemptuous with ar-
guments

guments againſt the children of God. Some in Paul's days pretended to love the ſame Saviour, preach the ſame doctrine that Paul did, and yet averred that he ſaid, *let us do evil that good may come.* The deſcription wiſdom gives of theſe is, they are ſaid to ſit at the doors, to call paſſengers who go right on their way, to be loud and clamorous, to watch for the ſaint's halting, to rejoice when their feet ſlip, to wait for iniquity, and never to reſt at quiet unleſs they have prejudiced or ſtumbled ſome one or other. *They ſleep not unleſs they have done miſchief, and their ſleep is taken away unleſs they have cauſed ſome to fall.* Prov. iv. 16.

The brutal fondneſs of theſe apes brought to my mind the way in which an hypocrite deceives and plunders a ſimple believer; there is hardly a ſincere ſoul that I know but in his infant ſtate of grace has fell a prey to theſe. When they have a mind to pick your pocket or *make a gain of you,* they generally take a glaſs or two of rum, brandy, or good old Geneva, and the operation of that, ſets all the bowels of candour to work; then they will pour you out a whole gill of tears; Joel well underſtood their way, *Awake ye drunkards, howl ye drinkers of wine,* Joel i. 5. and ſo they will until they have got the *baubees,* and then like the ape with the apple, they ſet off (as he does) upon the houſe top, chattering and bidding de· fiance to all the inhabitants within. Of this ſtamp were the multitude that followed the Saviour over the ſea of Tiberius for the loaves and fiſhes, whom

8   he

he fent back, telling them, they muft eat his fleſh and drink his blood, or die for ever. ·

An ape is very odious and dangerous to *pregnant women* ; bad effects have been known to have been produced from women in ſuch cafes taking fright at the fight of an ape, and furely nothing is more dangerous to a pregnant or fruitful church than a profound hypocrite, who hates the power of religion and the poffeffors of it ; by their hypocrify and their errors they have fome-times fo injured Zion, and even her paftors alfo, that her very offspring have appeared improper children, vifibly marked and chattering a wild gibberiſh, between Hebrew and Aſhdod, till fun-dry fiery trials have melted their fpirits, and the divine potter has put his hand a fecond time to this work on the wheels, and turned thefe ill-ſhaped veffels into a better form ; for as the *clay is in the hand of the potter fo are we in his hand,* and he does with us *as the potter does with his clay,* makes us fuch veffels as pleafe him, namely, vef-fels of honour ; and when done, *thofe that erred come to underſtanding, and thofe that murmured learn dcɛrine* ; fo that thofe marked ones which feemed to have the *face of an ox* come to appear with the *face of a man,* Ezek. 1. 10. when the *living creature* appears in the wheels. Ezek. x. 17.

I obſerved in the fchool of apes, that notwith-ſtanding all their likenefs to the human fpecies, their cunning, mimicry, and fondnefs, they were
all

all chained down to the floor, as not to be truft-
ed though in the precinƈts of the Tower; this
brought to my mind the ftate of hypocrites, who
notwithftanding their likenefs to real faints, their
cunning by which they deceive, their feeming
fondnefs of thofe they flatter, they are all bound
down; the *wicked is holden with the cords of his fin,*
fays Solomon. Some are tied down to *luft,* fome
to *coveteoufnefs,* fome to *envy* againft the faints,
fome to *errors,* and fome to the *dram* bottle, infomuch that the carbuncles of their face proclaim
the *good fpirit* of *candour* that ebbs and flows in
their bowels; the well-known cant of thefe is,
put *fugar* and *brandy,* but no *wormwood* nor *gall,* in
the miniftry of the word; all zeal, faithfulnefs,
reproof, warning, caution, and rebukes is father-
ed upon the fpirit of the devil, as if *Satan was
divided againft himfelf.* Thofe who make a gain of
godlinefs are noted for candour, and thofe that
God ufes to bring finners to Chrift are of the
fpirit of the devil; fo it was in the days of old,
*to Simon Magus they had all refpeƈt as the great
power of God.* Aƈts viii. 10. but Chrift, who de-
clared that hypocrites could not efcape the *damna-
tion of hell,* they called *Beelzebub the prince of devils.*
Thefe were of an open candid fpirit; they
preached one thing and lived another, as Peter
talks of fome who *promifed liberty to others while
themfelves are the fervants of corruption.* We read
of *prophets who prophefied of wine and ftrong drink.*
Mic. ii. 11. and no doubt but.fuch filled their
bottles

bottles by their pleafing candied prophecies, till they made fport of them that were prophets of the Lord, calling them fools, and *fpiritual men mad*, or influenced by a bad fpirit, Hof. ix. 7. David complains that he was the *fong of the drunkard*, Pfa. lxix. 11. However the hypocrites may get into the church, yet they are in bondage under the fentence of God, as well as to their own fin; hence we read of fuch, *who were of old ordained to this condemnation*, Jude 4.— Solomon *had a navy of fhips that came once in three years, bringing apes and peacocks*, 1 Kings x. 22.— but our eternal Solomon has no call to fend fo far for them; he has fcarcely a *palace* or a *lodge* in Great Britain where the ftewards of the houfe-hold are not complaining that they are over-ftocked with thefe hairy-ones.

I have fuch an averfion to apes, that I would fooner keep a ferpent or a fcorpion in my houfe than one of thofe creatures; and as a minifter, I would fooner preach to fifty carelefs unre-formed finners, who are called ferpents and vipers, than to a thoufand hypocrites, who fit under the gofpel for bafe ends, abandon them-felves to idlenefs, and by walking in craftinefs get a livelihood out of fimple people, or even ftand pimp for drunkards, rather than work with their own hands, and with quietnefs eat their own bread; thefe are enemies to God, ftrangers to the power of religion, and the experience of it on the heart of the righteous. The poor
feeker,

feeker, who is fenfible of his want—is of a teachable fpirit—waits at Wifdom's gate—efteems them that fear the Lord—favours the Saviour's righteous caufe—and longs for the manifeftation of pardoning mercy—I love, pity, and pray for; but idle, empty hypocrites I cannot away with; for their whole ftudy is to prejudice the minds of weaklings, and to injure the caufe of God; with thefe I truft I fhall ever carry on an offenfive and defenfive war; Chrift came not to fend peace between us and them, but a fword, therefore it is a juft and an holy war. Perhaps you will anfwer,

> Peace is thy calling, friend, not war;
> Doth not thy calling and contention jarr?
> 'Tis *holy war*—this makes the wonder ceafe;
> The fight of faith becomes a man of peace.

The *traitor's bridge and gate,* by which fome rebels came into the Tower to lofe their lives, put me in mind of the *arch-way* by which fome come into the church; and the *traitor's gate* that leads to the river, fhews the wide gate by which many hypocrites go out, who, as Paul fays, are *drowned in deftruction and perdition,* 1 Tim. vi. 9. Let this bridge and gate caution us againft the diffoyalty and rebellion of hypocrites; it is dreadful to a loyalift to be imprifoned (though but for a time) by the Great King—but it is a *fearful thing to fall into the* [revengeful] *hands of the living God,* Heb. x. 31. We faw

C the

the ax by which some lost their heads; but to miss of Christ, to lose the *head of the church*, is an infinite, irreparable, and eternal loss. The blackest character in the Bible (excepting Satan the prime leader of angelic sinners) is *Judas the traitor.*.

The *pieces of cannon* that are mounted around the Tower, put me in mind of some of our present *Boanergeses*, falsely so called, who deliver every message *from the mount that burns with fire, with blackness, darkness, and tempest, the sound of a trumpet, and the voice of words*, Heb. xii. 18, 19. The prophet Elijah, who travelled so far to pay his visit to Horeb, found the same earthquake, wind, and fire, as Moses had done, 1 *Kings* xix. 11.—a caution this to every believing soul not to attempt seeking the King of Zion at Sinai or Horeb. Moses put a vail on his face near this mount; and Elijah, who was the chariot and horsemen of Israel, was obliged *to wrap his head in his mantle*, when God demanded *What dost thou here Elijah?* 1 Kings xix. 13. The fiery law is to be handled, in order to alarm, rouze, shake, and awaken the drowsy, careless sinner; but if you batter his ears and entertain his mind with nothing but repeated rounds of fiery salutations, you will soon sear his conscience as with an hot iron, and make his heart cannon and bomb proof; and, like Job's *horse when his neck was clothed with thunder, he will paw in the valley*; and instead of being afraid or awed, *he will rejoice in his strength and go forth even to meet the armed men*, Job xxxix. 19—21.

" To

" To threats the ftubborn finner oft is hard,
Wrapt in his crimes againft the ftorm prepar'd;
But when the milder beams of mercy play,
He throws his garb, his cumbrous cloak away.
Thunder and lightning, heaven's artillery,
As harbingers before the Almighty fly;
Thefe but proclaim his ftile, and difappear;
The ftiller found fucceeds, and God is there."

The old fhattered and neglected *tower*, which
ftands at the remoteft part from the gate of entrance, and the lownefs when compared to the
white tower, brought to my mind our myftical
Babel builders, who, as the Saviour tells us, *are
intending to build a tower*, the top of which is to
reach heaven; like that which the antient towering fchemers, called by way of derifion *Babel
builders*, began in the plains of *Shinar*; but the
Saviour tells us fuch tower-builders fet not down
firft to count the coft; and for want of this they
began to build, as the Babel-builders did, *but
have not wherewith to finifh*; hence the Saviour
fays, the *beholders began to mock*, as the Trinity
did after Nimrod's architects had produced
the plan, and got the royal command for the
execution thereof: " Go to (faid the builders),
" let us make brick and burn them throughly.
" Go to, faid they, let us build us a city and a
" tower, whofe top may reach unto heaven, and
" let us make us a name, left we be fcattered
" abroad upon the face of the earth," *Gen.* xi. 4.
The Trinity adopts their language: " Go to

" (fays God), let us go down and there confound
" their language, that they may not underftand
" one another's fpeech," *Gen.* xi. 7.   This tower
was intended to exceed the rainbow, that was
not fufficient to fecure them againft a fecond
deluge; its top was to reach heaven—it was intended to get them a name, and to prevent their
being fcattered; but they left it unfinifhed; for
the Trinity had them in derifion, laughed at
their calamity, and mocked when their fear
came.   It is true they got a name, which will
laft as long as the world ftands; it will never be
forgot fo long as a falfe prophet or a legal work-
monger remains in the world; yea, even at the
day of judgment there will be a confounding of
the language of fome builders; but from this
the believer is fecured—*he is not to be afhamed or
confounded world without end,* Ifa. xlv. 17.   This
tower was firft erected in their imagination—*nothing will reftrain them,* fays God, *from that which
they have* IMAGINED *to do*; they were all bent
upon it, left they fhould be fcattered abroad;
but their unanimous precaution againft fepara-
tion was the caufe of their difperfion; *fo the Lord
fcattered them abroad from thence, and they left off to
build the city,* Gen. xi. 8. or, as the Pfalmift fays,
he fcattered thefe proud [ones] *in the imagination of
their hearts.*

 The *enfign ftaff* upon the Tower reminded me
of the *rod that came out of the ftem of Jeffe,* Ifa.
xi. 1.   " And this rod of Jeffe is to ftand for an
                                                    " enfign

" enſign of the people; to it ſhall the gentiles
" ſeek, and his reſt ſhall be glorious," Iſa. xi.
10. This ſtaff reminded me of union; before
the ſtandard the troops are ranged and muſtered;
and in defence of the Imperial colours they all
unite as the heart of one man; to the royal
ſtandard rebels are commanded to repair, as
ſoon as a proclamation of the royal favour is
proclaimed,—emblematical this of ſaints uniting
in one faith, hope, and ſpirit, and of loſt ſinners
coming over to him *who received gifts for the
rebellious, that the Lord God might dwell among
them,* Pſalm lxviii. 18.

The *flag* or *banner* may ſerve to remind us of
the *banner of everlaſting love* which is diſplayed
over the head of a young recruit when in the
rendezvous or *banqueting houſe,* Song ii. 4. to let
him know that he muſt engage in the *fight of
faith* as ſoon as the royal bounty is ſpent.

The *mint* and the *balances,* by which the coin
is tried and adjuſted, brought to my mind the
many counterfeit religions which paſs as current
in our days; ſome are ſaid to be impreſſed and
bear an *image that God will deſpiſe,* Pſa. lxxiii. 20.
others to receive the *mark of the beaſt,* Rev. xiii.
17. others a *countenance that witneſſeth againſt them,*
Iſa. iii. 9. others wear a *whore's forehead,* Jer. iii. 3.
but there are ſome who *bear the image of the
heavenly Adam,* Rom. viii. 29. 1 Cor. xv. 49. only
theſe will paſs for ſterling in the great day; all
muſt be put into the balances and tried; God

C 3 will

will take no man's word; many commend their own candid fpirit, but God will try them in the balances of the fanctuary: *All the ways of a man are clean in his own eyes, but God weigheth the fpirits,* Prov. xvi. 2. furely men of low degree are vanity, and men of high degree are a lie; to be laid in the *balances together they are altogether lighter than vanity,* Pfa. lxii. 9. In fhort, all that have not *Chrift in them the hope of glory,* will have TEKEL written on them—*weighed in the balances and found wanting,* Daniel v. 27.

The *Spanifh armory,* that contains the inftruments of torture and cruelty, the iron collar, the iron thumb-fcrews, the formidable tooth-pick, and their ftrange weapons that were taken from the formidable armada, brought to my thoughts the views that the children of Ifrael had when they faw the troops, troop-horfes, war-chariots, arms, and armour of Pharoah and his hoft, on the fhore of the *Arabian gulf,* after the King's predicted fuccefs and momentary triumph was ended : *I will purfue, I will overtake, I will divide the fpoil, my luft fhall be fatisfied upon them*; *I will draw my fword, my hand fhall deftroy them,* Exod. xv. 9. but *God blew with his wind, then they funk like lead in the mighty waters,* verfe 10. One *blaft of the breath of God's noftrils* got the victory; and it was but a puff from the fame almighty Conqueror that blafted this expenfive, deep-laid, and well-contrived expedition. The Pope's *blefling* and *crofs-keys* were no fecurity againft his

power,

power, who *rides on the heavens for our help, and in his excellency upon the skies,* nor is it likely they should, feeing it is predicted, that the pope himself shall be destroyed by a blast from the same quarter; *whom the Lord shall consume with the spirit of his mouth and destroy with the brightness of his coming.* 2 Theff. ii. 8.

The tower gates being kept shut until opened by a porter, serves to shew the way by which sinners enter the *gates of Zion;* it is by the king's leave thefe gates are open to any; if he iffues out a command to the contrary there is no entrance. The king of Zion does more; he not only grants, but gives orders; without his voice there is no admission; *to him the porter openeth,* and to none elfe; without a royal grant there is no entering *the straight gate* or getting within the inner walls of Zion; the hypocrite may grope for them *or go round about Zion, count her towers, mark her bulwarks, and confider her palaces.* Pfalm xlviii. 12, 13. and that is all, while the inhabitants of the citadel can triumph and fay, *This God is our God for ever and ever, and will be our guide even unto death.* Pfalm xlviii. 14.

The *warders* or *guardians* of the tower, who wear the king's livery, shew and explain the curiofities, detect idle and ill difpofed perfons attempting to enter, exhibited to my mind the duty of a gofpel minifter when clad with the *righteoufnefs of Chrift,* with the *garment of falvation,* and

with

with the *spirit of sanctification,* whofe bufinefs it is,
to fhew and explain the royal armory, and the
peculiar treafures of the great king; to make all
men fee what is the hope of our calling, and to
1eveal and make known *the fellowfhip of the myf-
tery,* things which have been hid for many ages
paft, but are now brought to light in a glorious
manner by the gofpel. It is the duty of gofpel
minifters to take up *ftrollers,* who are backfliding
and wandering from their refting place or out of
the way of underftanding; to take them up with
a royal warrant, bring them to the bar of confcience, appeal to truth againft their conduct, and
try them by the laws of Zion; the ancient watchmen ferved the fpoufe fo; *the watchmen that went
about the city found me.* Song iii. 3. She ftrolled
until fhe had loft fight of her royal confort, provoked him to jealoufy by her conduct, infomuch
as *fhe fought him but found him not, fhe called him
but he gave her no anfwer.* Song v. 6. She was
gone back to her *firft hufband the law,* Rom. vii.
3, 4. and had got the *old vail* on her face again;
therefore the *watchmen found her, they fmote her*
with the ftaff of authority, *they wounded her* with
the fword of the Spirit; *the keepers of the wall took
away her vail from her,* Song v. 7. and brought
her back with a *blufhing face,* covered with fhame
and confufion, to her much flighted Lord, from
w.or, without any provocation, fhe had treacher-
oufly eloped. Thefe warders take up idle pilfering perfons; fo minifters are to detect hypocrites,

crites, who under a maſk of religion, and by
making a falſe ſhew and an outcry about holineſs,
deceive the ſimple and live by ſacrilege, by rob-
bing the church of God, countenancing and
ſtrengthening the hands of evil doers. The apoſtle
had no ſmall trouble with theſe; *for we hear that
there are ſome which walk among you diſorderly, working not at all, but are buſybodies; now they that are
ſuch we command, that with quietneſs they work and
eat their own bread.* 2 Theſſ. iii. 11, 12.

The prophet Ezekiel, that watchman of Iſrael,
had no ſmall trials from ſacrilegious ladies;
" Likewiſe thou ſon of man ſet thy face againſt
" the daughters of thy people, which propheſy
" out of their own heart, and propheſy thou
" againſt them; and ſay, thus ſaith the Lord
" God, woe to the women that ſow pillows to all
" armholes. Will ye pollute me among my peo-
" ple for handfuls of barley, and for pieces of
" bread to ſlay the ſouls that ſhould not die, and
" to ſave the ſouls alive that ſhould not live, by
" your lying to my people that hear your lies;
" becauſe with lies ye have made the righteous
" ſad and ſtrengthened the hands of the wicked."
Ezek. xiii. 19—22. The work of theſe up-
holſterers, was making pillows for the armholes,
that is, bolſtering up hypocrites, looſe profeſſors,
and idle perſons; for which wickedneſs, the word,
or judgments of God often ſmote them, and they
beginning to ſink under the ſtroke, ran to one of
9 theſe

thefe ladies of candour, who told them that the man that rebuked them was not a prophet of a good fpirit but quite the reverfe, therefore not to be regarded; nothing but candour and fweetnefs could ever come from God, from his word, or from his Spirit, and with this *pillow*, the fmitten, blafted, withering, and finking hypocrite was propped up and fortified againft the fword of the Spirit, and thofe that handled it; fo that all re-proofs, rebukes, and fharpnefs, ufed againft an hypocrite, an idle profeffor, a bufybody, or a blowzy faced drunkard, is the effects of a bad fpirit, and not to be regarded. A minifter of Chrift is not to fpeak like the *piercing of a fword*, nor to ufe *fharpnefs*, left they roufe the fleepy or difquiet the carnally fecure profeffor; nothing but candour and fweetnefs is to be ufed; no zeal for God, no *difobedience is to be revenged*, no mumping hypo-crite is to be difcovered, nothing but bowels of mercy are to be put on by a fervant of the Lord; thus hypocrites are bolftered up and fortified againft the word of God, until, *being often reproved, they harden their own neck*, and are fuddenly *de-ftroyed, and that without remedy*. Prov. xxix. 1. This is the bufinefs of thefe propheteffes, the ob-jects of their hatred are the children of God; they are faid to make the *righteous fad*, to deftroy fouls that fhould not die, by hardening them againft all conviction; the end they aimed at was a livelihood, it was done for pieces of *bread and handfuls of barley*; the name of God was *polluted*,

the

the hands of evil doers *ftrengthened*, and the righteous oppofed, to indulge themfelves in idlenefs, get the name of a prophetefs, and to enfhrine themfelves in the houfe, pantry, pocket, and confcience of every poor purblind finner that received a *wound* or *ftripe* from his maker.

The fecret *watchword* put me in mind of the witnefs of God's Spirit in the hearts of the faithful. This is one fecret that is with the righteous, none know any thing of this but the armies of the Lord of Hofts; this *watchword* comes from the Captain of our falvation, it is whifpered to the heart of every good foldier of Jefus Chrift, and is kept a profound fecret in the camp of the faints; it can never be explained nor divulged by any adverfary or hypocrite in the world, neither the wicked nor the fool underftand this.

The *drawbridge*, which when drawn up cuts off all communication, brought to my mind the Saviour who is the only way to the Father, by venturing on whom, millions have gone fafely over the very verge of the bottomlefs pit, which ftill continues to bear all up and fafely over, who come by this new and living way; but the time will come when this bridge will be drawn up to heaven, the *mafter will rife up* and *fhut the door*; then all communication will be cut off, no more grace, mercy, or truth communicated to men, no more communicating troubles to God in prayer; the bridge is drawn and the waters of

wrath

wrath feparate; Lord! Lord! open to us, will be all in vain at that day. *The Lord forgave the iniquity of my fin,* faith the Pfalmift. *For this fhall every one that is godly pray unto thee, in a time when thou mayeft be found; furely in the floods of great waters they fhall not come nigh unto him.* Pfalm xxxii. 5, 6.

The bold attempt of *Colonel Blood,* who difguifed himfelf in the garb of a doctor of divinity, with a band, falfe band, a cap with ears, &c. &c. in order to get acquainted with the keeper of the *regalia,* who, with his accomplices knocked down the keeper with a mallet, feized the crown, fceptre, dove, &c. &c. and put them into a wallet in order to carry them off, but was difcovered and fecured before he could get out of the tower, brought to my mind the daring and prefumptuous claim that hardened hypocrites lay to the crown of loving kindnefs and tender mercy; who come into the church only to fpy out our liberty, mifufe the officers, encourage rebels in their wickednefs and lead them to deftruction. They cannot endure to fee the officers of Zion's king entrufted with fuch valuables; they covet the office and the honour of it; but they have no power from the king, therefore they hate and oppofe the power in others, and palm the devil, that actuates them, upon thofe that oppofe their hypocrify; and by thefe means they fupport the intereft of Satan and bring thoufands to his gloomy regions. *Jannes and Jambres, who withftood Mofes,*

Mofes, 2 Tim. iii. 8. did, by counterfeiting his power, render him in the eyes of Pharaoh no more than a magician, and the miracles of God, which Mofes wrought, were debafed to a level with magic or devilifh art. This was enough to harden the heart of Pharaoh and all his houfe till their country was ruined, the fiercenefs of God's wrath poured out, *evil angels were fent among them*, the firft born of man and beaft deftroyed, and Pharaoh and all his hofts overwhelmed in the Red Sea.

It was four hundred falfe prophets kept in idlenefs by *Ahab* that brought him to his deftruction ; thefe all *fpoke in the name of the Lord.* Jehofhaphat faid unto the king of Ifrael, *enquire, I pray thee, at the word of the Lord to-day* ; then the king of Ifrael gathered the *prophets together, about four hundred*, and faid, fhall I go againft Ramoth-gilead to battle, or fhall I forbear ? and they faid, *Go up, for the Lord fhall deliver it into the hand of the king.* And Jehofhaphat faid, is there not here a prophet of the Lord befides, that we might enquire of him ? And the king of Ifrael faid, *There is yet one man, (Micaiah the fon of Imlah) by whom we may enquire of the Lord; but I hate him, for he doth not prophefy good concerning me, but evil.* And Jehofhaphat faid, Let not the king fay fo. Then the king of Ifrael called an officer, and faid, *Haften hither Micaiah the fon of Imlah. And the meffenger fpake unto Micaiah, faying, behold now, the*
. *words*

words of the prophets declare good to the king with one mouth; there is not a bad fpirited man among them; every one is clothed with *bowels of mercy*, there is no *wormwood, bitternefs*, or *gall* made ufe of; nothing but *fweetnefs and candour* drops from their lips; let not thy bitter fpirit blaft the king's fcheme, nor dare to fet thy face againft an affemblage of four hundred prophets, who *prophefy good* with one confent; be intreated, lay by your fingularity; I fpeak as a friend, I know you are a prophet of the Lord, but you muft not prophefy againft thefe good men; thefe to a man have *prophefied good*; *let thy word, I pray thee, be like the word of one of them, and fpeak that which is* GOOD. 1 Kings xxii. 13. And Micaiah faid, *As the Lord liveth, what the Lord faith unto me, that will I fpeak.* Can this be the Spirit of the Lord? is it not the reverfe? So he came to the king, and the king faid unto him, *Micaiah, fhall we go againft Ramoth-gilead to battle, or fhall we forbear?* and he anfwered him, *Go, and profper, for the Lord fhall deliver it into the hand of the king.* Thefe were the words *verbatim* that were delivered by the four hundred good prophets. But yet this will not do; the king took it as a humorous jeft, and faid unto him, *How many times fhall I adjure thee that thou tell me nothing but that which is true in the name of the Lord?* This was intended to reprefent Micaiah as a lying prophet in the eyes of Jehofhaphat, though he had fpoken nothing but the very words which the *prophets of candour* had

dropped.

dropped. *And Micaiah said, I saw all Israel scattered upon the hills as sheep that had no shepherd; and the Lord said, these have no master* (their king was killed), *let them return every man to his house in peace.* And the king of Israel said to Jehoshaphat, *Did I not tell thee that he would prophesy* NO GOOD *concerning me, but* EVIL? And Micaiah said, *Hear thou therefore the word of the Lord; I saw the Lord sitting on his throne and all the hosts of heaven standing by him, on his right hand and on his left.* And the Lord said, *Who shall persuade Ahab that he may fall at Ramoth-gilead? and one said on this manner and another on that manner.*

Now we come to the *fountain head of candour*, where all false prophets and false prophetesses fill their pitchers, to supply and entertain the minds of a candid public. *And there came forth a spirit and stood before the Lord, and said, I will persuade him. And the Lord said unto him, wherewith? and he said, I will go forth, and I will be a lying spirit in the mouth of all his prophets; and he said, thou shalt persuade him and prevail also, go forth and do so.* This was the spirit that clothed them all with bowels of mercy, and that filled their hearts with that *candour* and *sweetness* which entertained not only the king and his nobles, but a candid public at large; they were in the sweetest union, unanimous in their predictions, and *prophesied* GOOD *with one* MOUTH. But Micaiah, with his rancour, spleen, and bitterness, persists in his singularity.

Now

Now therefore behold, the Lord hath put a lying spirit in the mouth of all these thy prophets, and the Lord hath spoken evil concerning thee. Who could have thought that a *lying spirit* could be in the *mouth* of four hundred prophets, whose mouth *prophe-sied nothing but good?* Here is Micaiah, who is said to *prophecy nothing but evil,* opposing four hundred prophets, who are said to prophesy good with one consent; now, how is a candid public to judge; why this pudding must be proved by its spending. If the good prophecies are true, the victory will be given to Ahab, and if Micaiah's evil prophecies be true, then Ahab loses his life and Israel is *scattered, having no master;* but as it may be some time before God decides the point, it will be necessary to give Micaiah a good drubbing, if it is but to caution others. *Then Zedekiah the son of Chenaanah went near and smote Micaiah on the cheek, and said, which way went the Spirit of the Lord from me to speak unto thee?* This man had got the *Spirit of the Lord,* according to his own account, and he prophesied good to a candid public; but as Micaiah did not belong to the public he had no part of the candour; all that he got was a knock on the head to extort a con-fession; *Which way went the Spirit of the Lord from me? and Micaiah said, behold, thou shalt see in that day, when thou shalt go into an inner chamber to hide thyself. And the king of Israel said, take Micaiah, and carry him back to Amon the governor of the city, and to Joash the king's son; and say, Thus saith the king,*

king, put this fellow in the prison, and feed him with bread of affliction and with water of affliction, until I come in peace. If Micaiah has nothing but these bitter herbs to live on till the king returns in peace, he will have a starving and long imprisonment. But the prophet knew better; *if thou return at all in peace, the Lord hath not spoken by me; and he said, hearken O people, every one of you;* read 1 Kings 22d chapter. Micaiah stuck to his text, and the Lord preached the sermon, the application of which was the death of Ahab, of Jezebel, of the royal family, and of all the prophets, who fell by the sword; and so they arrived at the eternal habitations, and in the good company of that *spirit* from which all their candour, sweetness, and good prophecies came. Thus it often happens that *men of candour* perish in their *sweetness,* while those that are said to *prophesy no good but evil,* prolong their lives and die in peace; and what shall we say to these things? why, if God be for these bitter prophets, who can be against them? Those that prophesied nothing but good to men, prophesied nothing but lies, and God was against them; the other prophesied nothing but evil, and yet he prophesied nothing but truth, and God was with him: therefore I conclude that it is better to prophesy evil by the Spirit of truth from God, though false prophets smite us and a candid public condemn us, than to prophesy good by the spirit of lies from the devil, though all the world approve and admire the moderation,

D   openness,

opennefs, fweetnefs, compaffionate bowels, tender
pity, and candid difpofition of the prophet; it is
not what men call good, for they fometimes *call
evil good,* Ifa. v. 20. but what God calls *truth, that
muft make people free.*

The *river Thames,* which is of ineftimable
worth to this metropolis, being compofed of
the Thame, the Ifis, Rickmanfworth, the
River Mole, &c. &c. may remind thee of that
river the ftreams whereof make glad the city of God,
Pfa. xlvi. 4. You may embark at the Tower
and fail to the Nore, to the Downs, and into the
Englifh channel, and fo round the world, if you
keep a proper diftance from the poles; nor will
you feel much want of either light or heat if you
keep under the torrid or temperate zone. So
every veffel of mercy that embarks in the *river
of the waters of life* fhall make a glorious and
eternal voyage; he fhall fail in his God, and end
in an eternity of pleafure that knows neither
bottom nor fhore; the river of regeneration (but
no other) leads to this: " There the glorious
" Lord will be to us a place of broad rivers and
" ftreams; wherein fhall go no galley with oars,
" neither fhall gallant fhips pafs thereby; then
" is the prey of a great fpoil divided, the lame
" take the prey; and the inhabitants fhall not
" fay I am fick; the people that dwell therein
" fhall be forgiven their iniquity." *Ifa.* xxxiii.
21. 23, 24.

This

This is the glorious end we have in view; pof-
feffed by our covenant head and reprefentative,
who in our nature, name, and perfons has taken
poffeffion, and appears in the prefence of God
for us, who are kept by almighty power through
faith to the fame. It is fecured by promife, by
oath, by covenant, by the blood of the teftator,
by the broad feal of heaven, and by the omnipotence and faithfulnefs of divine, immutable,
and infinite veracity; the firft fruits are gathered
by the hand of faith, and are a fatisfactory
earneft or fweet foretafte to the expectation of
hope; we are predeftinated and called, and fhall
therefore be glorified; we are ranfomed, and
fhall return with fongs and everlafting joy upon
our head, *Ifa.* xxxv. 10; we are enabled to believe, and fhall not be afhamed nor confounded
world without end; we are loved with an *everlafting love,* Jer. xxxi. 3. partakers of *everlafting
life,* John vi. 47. clothed with an *everlafting
righteoufnefs,* Dan. ix. 24. faved in the Lord with
an *everlafting falvation,* Ifa. xlv. 7. we fhine in
everlafting light, Ifaiah lx. 19. are heirs of an
eternal inheritance, Heb. ix. 15. and fhall poffefs
an *everlafting kingdom,* Pfa. cxlv. 13. O what has
grace done for us; we are wooed and efpoufed,
and fhall therefore be wedded and enjoyed; we
fhall bear the image and likenefs of our royal
head—poffefs a manfion of his own preparing—
and be no lefs than heirs of God and joint heirs
with the King of Kings, and Lord of Lords.

This world is our furnace, the angels are our guard, regeneration is our road, Chrift is our end, and heaven our home.

I hope thou wilt not be offended at this public prefent. I know alms ought to be given in fecret, but as thou art (through grace) a partaker of the promife, it is rather a prefent than an alms. You know I muft be employed about fomething; I hate idlenefs; I would fooner be what Elijah was—a zealous faithful troubler of Ifrael, than a candid fluggard, who will not lift his hand to his mouth. You would infift upon treating me with a fight of the curiofities of the Tower, and as a recompence I have fent you the few fpoils that I pilfered and pocketed from thence: one good turn deferves another; I have prefented to your view what you defired fhould be prefented to mine; and in order to pull down the price of feeing the Tower, the greateft part of its curiofities are here exhibited to a *candid public* at fo fmall a price as one fixpence—only for the fake of ready money.

With refpect to the fale of thefe curiofities, your affiduity, vote, intereft, and recommendation is expected. Advertifements in public newfpapers, bookfellers prefaces, outcries at places of public refort, or the vaporifh puffs of hawking pedlars, appear to me as fo many indications of the craftinefs of the trader, and the

worth-

worthleffnefs of the ftale commodity; ftinking
fifh require a loud and a lying cry,—they muft be
turned over in hafte before the cuftomer's eyes—
a large price fixed and infifted on—a deal of talk
in ftriking the bargain is required—and an hafty
flight, attended with a great noife, when the
commodity is delivered, left an hue and cry
fhould follow.

I was very forry at the report of thy ficknefs;
am thankful for thy recovery; this ficknefs has
not been unto death; all the time we gain by
trading there is no room for complaint, whether
we occupy bufinefs in deep waters or fuffer in
the furnace of afflidtion; every confeffion, peti-
tion, fupplication, interceffion, or tribute of
praife that is offered to God, has its promife in
the word of God, and will turn out to good
account at laft. It is better to live near the
Tower with a good hope through grace, than to
have the bounds of our habitation fixed in
Stationers Court, where there is *Creed Lane* at the
back, *Paternofter Row,* in the face, *Ave Maria
Lane* on the right hand, and *Amen Corner* at the
left. I would fooner find the bleffings of one
chapter of the Bible in my heart, than have poffeffion of the *Chapter Houfe*; it is better to have
Paul's God than to be Dean of *St. Paul's Church.*
I would fooner be bleffed with a good ftate of
health, than have the advice (gratis) of a college
of phyficians; a ufeful dodtor of divinity is bet-

ter than a doctor of phyfic; a man's fpirit will
fuftain the infirmities of the body, but a wounded
fpirit who can bear? Farewell; excufe hafte;
and believe me to be thy willing fervant, to ferve
thee with fuch as I have.

W. HUNTINGTON.

Dated from the Burning Bufh,
    April 10, 1788.

F I N I S.

www.ingramcontent.com/pod-product-compliance
Lightning Source LLC
Chambersburg PA
CBHW031803090426
42739CB00008B/1134